LIVING ON THE EDGE

Series Editor: MEIC STEPHENS

GOMER

S|L

First Impression—March 1996

ISBN 1 85902 305 3

© David L. Adamson

Printed in Wales by
J. D. Lewis, and Sons Ltd., Gomer Press, Llandysul, Dyfed

The intention of this essay is polemical: to sting a response from the various agencies of Welsh society which have an interest in the quality of life of the ordinary and less than ordinary Welsh people. The central thesis of the essay is a simple one: that the political life of Wales has become irrelevant to the lives of its people. Further, that Welsh political institutions and the people who run them are failing the population at large, which daily descends deeper into a culture of poverty and decline where aspirations are eroded and horizons are lower than at any time since the industrial communities of Wales came into existence. There is a crisis deep in the heart of Welsh society but no one speaks of it. There is a crisis which, if unresolved, will waste the lives of a substantial proportion of a generation of Welsh people. There is a crisis which no political party in Wales has fully recognized. Behind this failure lies a political bankruptcy; a bankruptcy of ideology and intellect which paralyses those sections of the Welsh social structure which have the capacity to fight for change. Wales has enjoyed several periods of radicalism in its history, but contemporary political organizations in Wales lack any form of radical vision and have descended into the most ineffective forms of constitutionalism and parliamentarianism. Wales and its people has become characterized by a slavish acceptance of the law and the confinement of the political process to the institutions of the local and central state.

This essay will establish the causes and nature of the crisis in Welsh society and analyse the reasons why the political process in Wales skirts around it. The political parties in contemporary Wales have failed to resist the steady erosion of the welfare state and fail to represent the interests of those who suffer the consequences of crisis. This essay will call for a new political agenda in Wales which will place the victims of crisis at its centre and mobilize demands for radical change.

The crisis: form and effects

One of the features of the crisis in Welsh society is its near-invisibility. You won't see it on the high street, you won't experience it at the local rugby-match. You won't find it at the out-of-town shopping-centre or the latest heritage museum celebrating Welsh tradition. You may see it shuffling along the street of a Valley town in a shabby track-suit and worn-out trainers or searching for bargains in Hypervalue and Pound Stretcher. You won't see it teeing-off on one of the host of new golf-courses which are appearing along the coastal belt in South Wales and you're unlikely to see it in St David's Hall or Theatr Clwyd. You will see it if you stand outside a comprehensive at 3.30pm or speak to the young people who congregate on street-corners in Porth or Bangor. This crisis is hidden from the eyes of mainstream Wales; from the traditionally affluent and educated élites who have been joined in recent years by a new-working-class which has benefited from the diversification of economic activity in Wales (Adamson, 1988).

The crisis is geographically and spatially specific. Endemic throughout Wales in both rural and urban locations, the crisis is a crisis of working-class communities. It is limited to the local authority housing-estates built in the post-war period. It is limited to those communities of Wales which have taken the brunt of the effects of the restructuring of the Welsh economy. This restructuring and diversification have been taking place throughout the post-war period but they have accelerated dramatically in the 1980s and 1990s. Some of these communities have suffered national and international ill-repute. Penrhys and Ely have become by-words for poverty and deprivation and a corresponding descent into lawlessness. New stereotypes of working-class life-style have replaced cloth-caps and allotments with images of joy-riding and delinquency. As with all stereo-types they hide a plurality of experience and life-style which include both socially legitimate and criminal responses to the crisis facing these communities. What is inescapable is that these communities are some of the most deprived in the European Community.

6

Characterized by high rates of unemployment and benefit dependency, these communities face processes which deny participation in the social, economic and political practices of contemporary society. Social exclusion (Williams, 1992) is a term gaining currency in European debates on poverty and deprivation. The term addresses the ways in which marginalized groups in society are excluded from full citizenship by informal and invisible forms of economic and social disadvantage. The term 'social exclusion' also enjoys some currency in debates on poverty in Britain. The Child Poverty Action Group defines poverty in terms of exclusion: 'people live in poverty when they are excluded from participating in the accepted ways of life in the society in which they live because of the low level of their resources.' (Oppenheim, 1993,p vii)

Combinations of poor education, ill-health, bad housing and unemployment prevent individuals and communities realizing their potential. They are caught in a spiral of deprivation which is self-reinforcing and extremely difficult to break free from. A generation of Welsh people are being born into social disadvantage which will ensure that they will under-perform at school, be unemployed or work in marginalized and low-wage employment, will live in some of the poorest housing in Europe and be prone to disease and ill-health. If I were writing about the 1930s these claims would cause little surprise; writing in the 1990s, they are a national scandal.

Another term enjoying currency in European debates is 'precariousness'. This term signifies the existence of groups in society who are at risk of slipping into permanent poverty and social exclusion. Many communities in Wales are precarious in this sense. Dependent on single-firm employment or bound to declining industries, such communities can be pitched into poverty and exclusion by the withdrawal of a single company from the region. Many individuals also hover just above the poverty-line: trapped in insecure forms of employment, they move in and out of jobs, in and out of debt and in and out of anxiety and despair. Of major importance is the social effect of exclusion and precariousness on the young. High aspirations are impossible in the face of communal experiences of the kind I am concerned with in this essay. In a recent study of career aspirations of 13-year-olds in four areas of Scotland, Furlong and Cartmel (1994) found a depression of educational aspirations and a 'relatively restricted range of occupational aspirations and expectations in comparison to other areas'. (p.21) These findings were for the area identified as Steeltown in their study, which shared many characteristics with areas in Wales where traditional dependency on a single industry has left high levels of unemployment in the wake of closure.

Educational motivation is minimal and children turn away from academic values to embrace the values of fatalism and helplessness. A sense of individual agency is impossible to acquire in places where the structural forces of society and economy come to focus in a crushing sense of hopelessness. The traditional ability of the working-class to seek and demand change for itself has been eroded and weakened by legislative, political and social change. Communities which were highly organized and politically powerful are increasingly marginalized and disenfranchized as the occupational basis of their historical organization is eradicated.

At this stage of my argument I can envisage the eyes of the 'haves' beginning to glaze in the face of yet another plea on behalf of the 'have nots'. The invisibility of the crisis makes it easy to brush aside. If we are not confronted with it we have no need to think about it. This indifference is a sin of omission which can be counteracted by drawing attention to the plight of communities experiencing deprivation and social exclusion. More worrying is the disbelief with which claims such as these are frequently met. Many people assume that the welfare state is a barrier against poverty and that no one in Britain will face serious deprivation without the intervention of the appropriate authorities. This may have been true of the 1960s, the 'golden age' of welfarism in Britain, but it no longer is the case. Erosion of the value of benefits, changes from Social Security benefits to repayable loans and the virtual demise of social housing have ensured a collapse of the welfare systems which protected the working-class community I grew up in the 1950s and 1960s. The problem is most acute for the young who are denied benefit and remain dependent on families who frequently have no capacity to fund their existence beyond a depressing minimum. However, more worrying than the belief that poverty no longer exists is the increasingly popular practice of claiming that that the poverty and social exclusion is the result of failings on the part of the poor themselves.

Blaming the poor for their poverty is not new in Britain. The nineteenth-century Poor Law clearly distinguished between the deserving and undeserving poor, but strategies for transferring culpability to the poor have become increasingly sophisticated in the era of the New Right. Academics have identified the existence of an 'underclass'. In the analysis of Charles Murray (1989) the 'underclass' exists because it has a different value system from mainstream society characterized by criminality, fecklessness and sexual immorality. For Murray the plight of America's urban poor has nothing to do with unemployment, poor housing, inadequate education or poor health. It is a direct consequence of the reluctance to work, the easy acceptance of criminal behaviour and the level of illegitimacy in the poor communities. Economic causes of poverty are rejected in favour of cultural causes which effectively blame the poor for their own social exclusion and marginalization. Ideas such as these are attractive to the politicians of the New Right and deflect attention from the failure of the market system to trickle wealth into the areas of urban decay. They serve the purpose of suggesting a futility in providing welfare support. The poor are poor through choice and through their own failure to integrate with the life-style of the liberal market economies.

These theories, born in prejudiced analysis of America's urban ghettos, have been transferred to analysis of the poor in Britain. Notably *The Sunday Times* has propagated the use of the term to describe Britain's poor (Mitchell, 1994). Such theories brush aside the consequences of unemployment for the creation of poverty and deny the causal links between loss of income from work and poverty (Gaffikin and Morrisey, 1992). The following section of this essay will first establish the extent and nature of poverty and social exclusion in Wales and secondly demonstrate that the causes lie firmly with the economic restructuring of Wales and not in the actions and inaction of the poor themselves. Assumptions of this kind are the greatest barrier to resolving the crisis in Welsh society and need to be vigorously denied.

Poverty and social exclusion in Wales

The proof of the existence of alarming levels of poverty and deprivation is not difficult. I shall begin with some simple facts. I have drawn figures from Mid Glamorgan to illustrate my claims but they could have equally been drawn from Clwyd or Gwynedd. I have suggested that the key factor in the triggering of social exclusion is unemployment. Since the beginning of the 1970s there has been a steady rise in unemployment to reach levels which would have been considered unacceptable in the early post-war period. Central government in the Thatcher and Major years has abandoned any attempt to secure full employment and there is a general acceptance that full employment is no longer a realizable political objective (Gaffikin & Morrisey 1992). Politically in Britain there has been a desensitization to the plight of the unemployed and a readiness on the part of many sections of society, including the working-class, to blame the unemployed themselves for their condition. If we begin with the early 1970s we see that in 1971 the UK unemployment rate was 3.1%, the rate for Wales was 4.0% and the rate for Mid Glamorgan was 4.7%. By 1980 the general rise in unemployment levels had raised those figures to 8.1%, 11.3% and 12.9 % respectively (*Digest of Welsh Statistics*). High levels of unemployment maintained themselves through the short-lived boom of the late 1980s and, even now as Britain is said to be coming out of the recession, the rate of unemployment is falling only slowly. The UK and Wales rate of unemployment in late

1993 coincided at   12.1 %, and for Mid Glamorgan 15.1% (*Employment Gazette*).   Such a simple statistic hides a range of features of the pattern of unemployment which are of crucial significance in identifying the precarious communities in our society.

First of all we have to be aware of the piecemeal legislative changes which have been made to definitions of unemployment which make historical comparison difficult. Changes to Department of Employment and Department of Social Security procedures removed many thousands of people from the unemployment register in Britain. The Unemployment Unit has identified a series of changes throughout the 1980s which have removed over one million claimants from the unemployment register (Unemployment Unit, 1986 &1988). As a consequence, the actual levels of unemployment are considerably higher than official statistics suggest. One means of overcoming this limitation is to consider the levels of economic activity in a community. Between 1981 and 1991 the levels of male economic activity in Mid Glamorgan fell from 74.06% of the male population of working age to 65.86%. Much of this decrease is found in those under 20 and those over 40. This uneven distribution of economic inactivity in the population creates specific effects with key age-groups finding increasing difficulty in securing work. Young, poorly qualified people and men shed from the traditional industries form a core of long-term unemployed which cannot be disguised by cyclical participation in government training-schemes. Additionally, one of the largest increases in the categories of economically inactive males has been in those registering permanently sick, fuelling speculation that Government strategy has encouraged the transfer of many unemployed people off the unemployment register onto invalidity benefit.

The second feature of this unemployment is its spatial organization. Driving along the M4 corridor in South Wales and the A55 express route in North Wales visitors could be impressed by the diversification of the Welsh economy and the host of retail parks and manufacturing centres. Yet twenty miles inland they would recognize the superficiality of the changes. Outside of the travel-to-work areas of these nodes of economic change the demise of traditional industries has left whole communities without an economic base. Additionally, the diversification of the economy has not created work for the workers shed by the heavy primary industries which made up the Welsh economy for most of this century. Jobs in electronics, textile and light manufacturing have frequently been perceived by all parties as jobs for women. This and the increase in the service sector has led to the impression that the Welsh labour market has become feminized with more women economically active than men. Teri Rees has done much to dispel this myth (Rees & Fielder, 1992) pointing to the reality of part-time, casualized labour carried out for low wages in the new industries of the Welsh economy. Participation in employment of this kind brings about its own patterns of precariousness and social exclusion which compound the poverty and deprivation of the working-class communities of Wales. Such work is almost invariably low-paid with the average wage in Wales being only 80% of the UK average.

The working-class communities of North and South Wales have been devastated by the pattern of unemployment discussed here. In the 1991 Census, wards with rates of male unemployment of slightly under 50% can be found, predictably located on housing-estates which additionally demonstrate other indicators of poverty and deprivation. The clustering of unemployment and low levels of economic activity is quite startling. Even within district authority areas huge disparities can be found with some Enumeration Districts in the 1991 Census recording 100% unemployment. The percentage figure here is less important than the realization that in small localities of up to thirty houses all the males are economically inactive. A young person growing up in such a locality may not directly know anyone who works for a living. The clearest pattern is the coincidence of unemployment black-spots with the large council estates of the post-war period.

However, even within this specific context, spatial difference exists with heightened problems in the 'new' estates built in the 1960s which are more readily characterized by decaying housing conditions, high density housing distribution and concentrations of isolated young families trapped in difficult-to-let properties. This peculiar spatial organization of unemployment and its effects ensures that the crisis it constitutes remains invisible for the remainder of the population who have no cause to visit the localities affected.

Finally, in considering the pattern of unemployment in Wales attention must be paid to its distribution in the age structure. Brief mention has been made of the way the burden of unemployment falls heaviest on two age categories: the young of both sexes and middle-aged men. The young in Wales have suffered below-average levels of educational attainment in Britain throughout the post-war period. Their ability to compete in the UK labour market is consequently restricted even if the cultural reluctance for labour mobility could be overcome. In terms of the local labour market long-term youth unemployment is endemic. Patterns have emerged where young people alternate between periods of unemployment, attendance on government training-schemes and employment in low-wage, temporary or casual positions. The result is an economic precariousness and a lack of any sense of security which allows long-term planning and financial commitment. For males over fifty the problem is equally acute as they have found themselves virtually unemployable in a changing economy which demands skills they do not possess and which favours the employment of women before men. The collapse of steel and coal has reduced a pool of traditionally skilled and highly organized labour to an acutely marginalized status in contemporary Welsh society.

Unemployment and social crisis

Unfortunately, unemployment does not travel alone; it brings with it a host of additional deprivations. The communities affected by unemployment demonstrate a failure to meet the

13

accepted standards of living of our society in almost every respect. The quality of housing, car ownership, access to public amenities and the ownership of basic domestic appliances are amongst the lowest in Europe. More fundamentally, the incidence of illnesses such as lung and respiratory disease, heart-attack and stroke, and diabetes, are amongst the worst in the western world. Educational attainment is the lowest in Britain and the rise of numbers of emotionally disturbed children in schools in these communities is resulting in an increasing practice of permanent exclusion, effectively denying education to those who need it most.

The highest levels of unemployment also coincide almost perfectly with the highest rates of lone-parenthood in the communities of Mid Glamorgan, a pattern which is demonstrated elsewhere. In Britain as a whole eight of the ten counties with the highest rates of unemployment also featured in the ten with highest levels of lone-parents (1991 Census). In Mid Glamorgan only two of the highest twenty-five wards for lone-parents had below the average rate of unemployment for the county. At district and ward level there is a high correlation between the levels of unemployment and lone-parenthood in communities. This is particularly evident when unemployment of males under thirty is considered. This statistical relationship does not necessarily demonstrate the existence of a causal relationship between the two factors although interview data does suggest there is one. What it does tell us is that the areas of highest unemployment are also characterized by a number of additional features of poverty associated with lone-parenthood and its inevitable high levels of benefit dependency.

Lone-parenthood has been blamed by politicians and analysts for almost every ill in our contemporary society. The now infamous speech by John Redwood (1993), Secretary of State for Wales, about 'single parents' on the St Mellons estate in Cardiff encapsulates the Government's attitude to one-parent families as both cause and symptom of declining social responsibility in Britain today. In a controversial report by Dennis and Erdos

14

(1992) the decay of working-class communities and rising rates of crime within them are clearly blamed on the demise of the traditional couple family and its replacement by the lone-parent family. For Dennis and Erdos the existence of 'families without fathers' is the source of changed social attitudes to family and a collapse of the traditional social control mechanisms of working-class communities. The absence of a male role-model in working-class homes has, for them, lead to a breakdown in the transmission of traditional values between generations. For them, rising crime is not a consequence of poverty, unemployment and lack of opportunity; it is a clear consequence of the absence of fathers in working-class families.

Research currently being conducted by the Regional Research Programme at the University of Glamorgan indicates otherwise. A more likely mechanism is the break-down of traditional rites of passage to adulthood. The high rates of unemployment and the lack of opportunity for young men have effectively abolished traditional routes into adulthood and its associated responsibilities. Traditional patterns of early school-leaving, early courtship and marriage, and early parenthood, have been broken. Without income, house purchase is impossible and the limited availability of social housing in the wake of council house sales ensures the social exclusion of the poor from any form of housing market. Without work and housing, men are unable to offer the financial security marriage in traditional working-class communities once offered. The attraction of a greater degree of independence for women as benefit claimants is challenging the automatic expectation of working-class women that they should marry early. Marriage as a rite of passage into adulthood for men and women is rapidly disappearing for the socially excluded and poor in Wales. The alternative pattern emerging is one of serial relationships which see the woman primarily responsible for any children resulting from the relationship. The claim here is that this pattern is a direct consequence of the poverty, social exclusion and precariousness of life in working-class communities. The

15

increase in lone-parent families is a symptom and not a cause of decay in working-class communities.

However, it is necessary to recognize the effects of the decline of traditional patterns of transition to adulthood. The effect of early marriage on young male working-class behaviour has traditionally constituted an effective means of social control. The early acceptance of the responsibilities of marriage and parenthood inevitably modified behaviour. The absence of such a transition to adulthood inevitably has removed some restraints on behaviour in working-class communities and has contributed to the rising levels of crime. This is clearly an indirect consequence of the effects of unemployment and social exclusion in communities which offer no legitimate alternative to paid employment as a means of livelihood.

The issue of rising crime has dominated home affairs in British politics for much of the last decade. Initially the property of the New Right, perceptions of rising crime-rates are now more universally accepted. For the Left in Britain during the 1980s rising crime was a figment of the Conservative imagination and a consequence of ideological redefinition of traditional working-class behaviour. However, there has been a slow recognition that there is a real rise in the incidence of criminal activity associated with young working-class males living in the deprived areas. What has been slow to develop is a Left critique of the situation which identifies the source of this behavioural shift in the policies and philosophy of the New Right itself.

Such a critique is not difficult to assemble. The first point which must be made is that the level of unemployment does have a causal relationship with the crime-rate. Direct demonstration of a link between unemployment and crime is notoriously difficult. The Government has clearly and categorically denied such a link, despite claims to the contrary from agencies active in crime prevention and victim support, including the Church of England. No one would claim that there exists a direct link which forces all unemployed people to commit crimes. However, it does seem simple commonsense that localities with few

legitimate opportunities for self-advancement and characterized by low self-esteem, frustrated ambition and low expectations will manifest a code of behaviour which has at its centre values which differ from mainstream culture and which demonstrate hopelessness and nihilism. The crimes of car-theft, joy-riding, burglary and vandalism which characterize the rising crime practices in such localities are precisely the kind of crime that such commonsense assumptions might predict.

More scientific evidence of a link between unemployment and crime has been provided by a major study based at Cambridge University (Wells, 1994 & 1995). Wells suggests that the failure of Home Office research to recognize a link between unemployment and crime lies in its failure to recognize unemployment as a 'lagging' indicator of crime levels. Wells suggests that abundant evidence exists for a clear link between the business cycle and levels of property crime but that Home Office research fails to recognize that unemployment lags behind the business cycle and consequently blurs the statistical correlation. Wells concludes: 'The fact is the nation's unemployment black spots ..... are also its crime black spots.... The reason our great urban conurbations are the nation's crime spots reflects poor regional/national economic performance, particularly rapid de-industrialisation in recent years.'(1995, p6).

This evidence does much to dispel Government rhetoric about rising crime as a symptom of moral decline and inadequate punishment, and clearly lays the blame for the rising rates of property and car-crime at the door of unemployment and the failure of the New Right to see the securing of higher levels of employment as a legitimate and necessary concern of government.

There is an additional component of the New Right contribution to the rising rate of crime in working-class communities. The celebration of the enterprise culture and the influence of market-forces has penetrated deeply into young working-class consciousness. Whilst the traditional political collectivism of the working-class has often been exaggerated, the

17

generally collectivist value system of working-class communities is an established social fact (Bott 1971, Goldethorpe et al, 1968). Strong family and community networks, clear patterns of socialization in work and trade unions and the influence of peer behaviour have conventionally ensured that working-class behaviour is modified in the interests of significant others. This form of collectivism has been an important regulator of the excesses of behaviour in working-class communities and traditionally has ensured that crime is not generally committed against the home community. However, fifteen years of individualist ideology in a wide range of social contexts has done much to erode this intrinsic set of collectivist behaviour patterns. The demise of collectivized experience in work-place cultures such as mining, coupled with the decline of the corresponding political organizations of trade unions and popular Labour Party membership, have been a secondary feature of the decline of the traditional industries in South and North Wales.

Changes in the school curriculum and a wider influence of business people in school management have ensured the trickling down of enterprise and individualist values in school culture. Children participate in enterprise activities which teach business values which cut across the core value system of working-class communities. The New Right has achieved a strategy which propagandizes possessive individualism in the most pervasive manner. Additionally, the leisure patterns of working-class communities have become more individualized and the general emphasis on consumption in society has raised aspirations without raising incomes. The consequences are a ready acceptance on the part of working-class youth to lay claim to the benefits of the consumer society with little reflection on the methods by which the benefits are accrued.

ESRC-sponsored research by Dr John Beynon at the University of Glamorgan clearly indicates an entrepreneurial culture in the violent young men interviewed as part of a project on violent male culture in South Wales. Many offenders saw themselves as fulfilling the values of Thatcherism and saw no

18

contradiction in their use of violence as a means to achieving the valued goods of a consumer society. The politics of possessive individualism which have characterized Britain since 1979 have inevitably devalued the traditional collectivist ethos of working-class communities. The consequence is that the vast majority of property crime is experienced by the poor as a result of the actions of their neighbours and peers (Wells 1995). The young working-class male perpetrates the majority of his crimes against his own community.

Often linked with discussions of crime is the related issue of drug-abuse. One clear consequence of the excluded life-style of the working-class estates in Wales is the response in terms of drug-abuse as a palliative for the poor quality of life which such locations offer. Interviews with agencies in South Wales suggest significant changes to the pattern of drug use in the 1990s. Use of cannabis has escalated from unproblematic leisure use to habitual and routine use as a tranquillizer. Additionally, prescribed tranquillizers are traded freely and the use of amphetamines has grown considerably. Of greater concern is the increasing supply of cocaine, its derivatives, and heroine, often at prices which reflect local incomes. Again, these problems are clearly associated with key housing-estates in the region. Taff Ely Borough Council in Mid Glamorgan recognizes drug-related crime as the most serious problem on its housing-estates and now pursues a policy of eviction for convicted drug-dealers.

The discussion of poverty in this essay has in many ways been abstract. The statistics and social trends examined are one step away from the daily reality of poverty in Wales. Poverty has to be lived to fully understand its nature. The experience of poverty is varied and influenced primarily by the life-stages individuals move through. From deprived childhoods to cold and hungry old age, sections of the population in Wales will spend a lifetime in poverty. No statistics can measure the frustration, powerlessness and lost opportunities of such a waste of human resources. Discussions with agencies working with the poor in Wales paint a depressing picture of a numbing life-style without hope or enjoyment.

That picture is of a constant struggle to make ends meet. Families with children exist on a daily income of as little as £2.50 after housing cost. The constant juggling of limited financial resources absorbs all the efforts of the waking day and saps energy. The burden of debt prevents forward planning and ensures that meagre incomes are substantially committed to clearing past expenditure whilst building new debts in the present. Once in this situation the poverty trap ensures that the poor pay more for almost every aspect of their consumption. Heating, food, clothing and transport all cost more when the individual is excluded by low income from the retail revolution which has swept Wales in the 1980s. Poor families are excluded from sources of credit and thrown into the hands of money-lenders who prey on the deprived estates in Wales. To live in poverty is to live in fear of eviction and repossession. It is to live with the threat and reality of disconnection of vital services such as water and electricity. It is to live in fear of the next knock on the door.

For the young living in poverty in Wales, the life is one without horizons and with limited ambitions. Trapped in communities without employment and with no social facilities, it is a life of drift and decline. Street-corners and empty houses offer gathering places where the inevitable companions are alcohol, drugs and solvents and a slide into petty-crime and delinquency. In a world without jobs other sources of identity and status come to the fore and are defined by the distorted values of the criminal sub-culture which inevitably emerges. Stealing and driving fast cars becomes a way of stating transition to manhood and maintaining a place in the local social hierarchy. Denied the transition to adulthood traditionally offered by work and marriage, young working-class males have established their own value-system which centres on violence and machismo and is now likely to permanently feature in the culture of the region.

Even now a return to full employment is unlikely to undo the damage of twenty years of economic decline.

The powerlessness experienced by the poor is overwhelming. The poor have virtually no arena where they can actively make decisions over the course of their lives. Income is committed before it is received and almost every aspect of their lives is determined by the officials who administer the benefit systems, the employment exchange, the training scheme and the local authority housing. The limited stability they experience can be jeopardized or lost by the decision of a bureaucrat in any of the departments they constantly have to negotiate with to secure their daily requirements. The rules of the benefit system effectively preclude education, training and voluntary work and individuals slip into a fatalism and passivity which compounds the hopelessness of their situation.

The effects on health of a life of poverty are incalculable. Physical health deteriorates early in the face of poor diet and reliance on cheap, high-fat sources of energy. Several studies have demonstrated that people in Britain today regularly experience hunger as a result of lack of money to buy food. Diseases of poverty and malnutrition are returning to the communities of Wales, exemplified by a noticeable increase in the incidence of tuberculosis. Alcohol and cigarette consumption are an inevitable by-product of the powerlessness and hopelessness of the life-style described by the agencies working with the poor communities. Tranquillizer dependence is endemic and little official attempt has been made to map the extent of illegal drug-use. The poor are excluded from life itself; they will die younger and experience poorer quality of life in the face of higher incidences of ill-health and incapacity. The levels of those registered permanently sick have risen constantly throughout the last decade.

One thing more than any other characterizes life for the poor in the 1990s in comparison to the past; the awareness of exclusion is highly developed in those who are excluded. The poor live in a society which is replete with the imagery of affluence and wealth, and poverty in the 1990s is exaggerated by the inequality which has developed with it. The socially excluded are conscious and aware of the benefits of life in an affluent society which they are prevented from enjoying. The Rowntree Foundation Inquiry into Income and Wealth (1995) has left no doubt as to the increasing polarization of British society since 1977. Following a brief postwar period when income and wealth converged, the trend since 1977 is for the poor to become poorer and the remainder of society to become more affluent. The pervasive influence of the visual media has ensured that the poor are bombarded daily with knowledge of their poverty and exclusion, leaving them alienated and detached from a commitment to the society which excludes them.

This unemployment crisis has been demonstrated to trigger a more serious social crisis with a web of deprivation and exclusion. The high level of unemployment is tearing at the fabric of working-class communities in ways which have consequences for all of Welsh society. These communities have constituted the backbone of Welsh society in the nineteenth and twentieth centuries. They have added a cultural diversity which has ensured the survival of a Welsh identity which moves beyond the limited consideration of language and Cymric tradition which form the basis of the 'imagined community' (Anderson, 1983) of the Welsh middle-classes, the Welsh-speaking literati and intelligentsia. The dynamism of working-class culture has structured the politics and the culture of Wales and given it a radicalism and a world-wide reputation for community and mutual aid. It is these characteristics of our working-class communities which are being destroyed by the process of unemployment and social exclusion. In their place is left a weakened and struggling communalism and a highly atomized and individualized culture. The experience of poverty is an isolated one. Communal responses are few and far between and the fabric of communities is under great stress. We must act before that fabric is torn asunder.

Towards the formation of a new politics

The solution to the crisis I have identified has to be a political solution. Wales has suffered acutely from the effects of fifteen years of New Right politics. A radical programme of political change is required to reverse those effects and to secure a new platform for the modernization and development of Welsh society. The scale of the problem to be tackled requires a radical rethink of the politics of the whole post-war period which have allowed the gradual return to the conditions which the 1945 Labour Settlement claimed to eradicate. British social democracy has failed the people of Wales and a new politics is required if there is to be any quality in the Welsh way of life in the new century.

The first requirement of any new basis for radicalism in Wales must be the realization that the process affecting the communities of Wales, even in the most rural enclaves, are the consequences of global events and practices. Wales cannot be seen as separate and distinct from the economic forces which create similar effects in Taiwan or the Basque region, Portugal or Arkansas. The villages of Wales are embedded in a world capitalist economy which shifts Japanese television production to Mid Glamorgan and imports coal through Cardiff docks from South Africa. We can afford no sense of independence from these processes and our political programmes must recognize and ameliorate their effects. We must be armed with an acute knowledge of the place of our nation within this global economic framework. Additionally, the politics of Wales are caught up in the global ideological struggles which have characterized world politics in the post-war period. Only through recognizing this global context and by working through its consequences can a new form of politics be found. The global issues must be addressed before the local difficulties can be resolved.

It is in this ideological arena that much of the struggle must take place. One of the major difficulties preventing the emergence of a new form of politics in Wales, and more generally on a global scale, is the ideological effects of the

23

collapse of the Soviet Union and its subject states. The revolutions which swept through Eastern Europe in the closing years of the 1980s have thoroughly redefined the political agenda in the western world. The collapse of the major ideological opponent of western liberal democracy has successfully removed key terms from the political vocabulary. Words such as socialism, equality and liberty have become identified with a failed and badly tainted social experiment. The worst excesses of the various Soviet-style regimes have been presented as a powerful demonstration of the intrinsic dangers contained within the philosophy of socialism as a doctrine. Western liberal democracies have engaged in a triumphalism about the end of struggle between socialism and capitalism. Events in Tianamen Square have highlighted the evil nature of the surviving communist regimes and any form of socialist project is deemed guilty by association. Claims have been made that western liberal democracy is now established as the final version of human consciousness and that it has established a permanent global consensus for the principles of the market-place. Francis Fukuyama (1989) exemplifies such claims in his perceptions about the 1989 revolutions signifying an end to the ideological struggles which have characterized history. For him Western democracy will be the final form of human government.

Not content with such a resounding victory over its long-standing ideological opponent, the triumphant victor stands astride its body and declares a war on history. Theories of post-modernism emerge to declare that the root of the evils of socialism are to be found in the Enlightenment project itself. For three hundred years we have mistakenly placed our faith in the power of human reason. A 'grand narrative' has been followed which bound us to unrealizable ideals which themselves have created human misery. It is claimed we have mistakenly thought that we understood the world and that we could, as a result, change it for the better. The knowledge we have of the world has been shown to be fallacious and the source of mistaken attempts to engineer social progress. Indeed, the concept of progress itself

24

has been challenged and set aside and parity claimed for all systems of thought. The attempt to promote socialism over capitalism is presented as a mistake of history which can only be redressed by accepting the chaos of the market-place and the struggle of everything against everything.

I shall not be concerned here to develop a critique of the excesses of post-modern epistemology. Its relativism and, at times, absurd reductionism are self-evident. However, I shall simply re-assert the belief that the world can be understood, that there is meaning to be derived and that it is possible to communicate and share that meaning. The result is an ability not simply to understand the world but to change it in ways we choose. However, the postmodern writers have forced us to recognize that the world is constantly changing and a 'truth' written over one hundred years ago is not necessarily true now. Similarly, theories which were meaningful in the early development of the industrial revolution are not necessarily of value today. The strategies of change we adopt must be informed by the past but they must be a product of the present, rooted in the social and economic conditions of our times. We must develop a progressive strategy which is possible to sustain and which does not appeal to a terminology and a doctrine which no longer reflect reality.

We must begin by challenging the ways in which the core doctrine of socialism has been ridiculed and de-legitimized as a strategy for the improvement of human existence. The principles of socialism are regarded as naive and utopian in the face of the reality of human existence which is perceived as inevitably 'nasty, brutal and short'. Claims of the existence of altruism and self-sacrifice are denied in the face of possessive individualism and the triumph of the market competitive ethic. How can a new politics, which places centrally the poor and the socially-excluded, emerge in such a hostile environment? How can those concerned with redressing gross inequality and the waste of human potential struggle against the apparent victory of a social system which produces poverty as one of its necessary by-products?

The starting-point has to be with issues of morality. Those who retain a sense that some of the features of the Enlightenment project remain valid objectives for a progressive society must begin to reclaim a sense of morality for those objectives. Those who feel that the existence of poverty can be objectively verified and that such an existence ridicules the claims to democracy made by liberal capitalist societies must reassert a critique of the morality of free enterprise capitalism. Those who feel that the international swings and roundabouts of the capitalist world economy exploit and discard whole nations at will must propagate a sense of outrage at the human misery left in the wake of wholesale movements of capitalist production.

It must be clearly demonstrated that liberal democracy fails in its own project of providing liberty and democracy for its citizens. The detailed practices of social exclusion given earlier in this essay demonstrate the failure of full active citizenship to be achieved by significant proportions of the population in Wales and in the other liberal democracies of Europe. Within the European Union, 50 million people are living in poverty (Williams, 1992). This invalidates any claim that liberal democracy might make to be the highest form of human government. It must be demonstrated that such liberal democracies fail in their ability to provide the welfare rights of employment, good housing, effective education and efficient health-care which must be seen as the most basic and fundamental rights in all societies. Without them the ability to participate as citizens in the practice of political and civil rights is meaningless. The ability of an illiterate to vote is the negation of political freedom and the meaningful participation of unemployed and poverty-stricken individuals in the benefits of contemporary society is impossible. The partial citizenship of all those affected by poverty and its consequences negate the very concept of democracy which is at the heart of the liberal democratic philosophy. The new politics must emphasize the right to participate and advance a programme for democracy with a real level of devolved responsibility to local decision-making bodies. Political participation must once again become a right which is valued and an obligation which is fulfilled. To secure the reinsertion of political participation into popular culture requires the propagation of a view that participation produces results. It requires a reconnection of political participation with influence over decision-makers at both local and national level. The more power is devolved to local institutions the more likely such a culture is to re-emerge. Wales needs a new sense of freedom with which to motivate the excluded.

Unfortunately, the opposite has occurred. The ascendancy of the New Right has seen a return to the narrow economic freedoms of classical liberalism. The philosophies of Hayeck have triumphed over the philosophy of Beveridge. In Hayeck's view the state's acceptance of any responsibility for welfare provision signals the end of freedom as it inevitably ties the state to satisfying the insatiable demands of society for such provision. Thus begins a slide towards totalitarianism as the state develops the necessary planning mechanisms to organize the welfare state and negates freedom through its taxation of economic activity (Hayeck, 1944). The only freedoms guaranteed in the contemporary philosophy of the market-place are the freedom to accumulate wealth and to retain it without state interference. This has been demonstrated most clearly in the controversy over salaries for the heads of the newly privatized public utilities. One of the most offensive examples has been evident here in Wales with the vast salary increases of Welsh Water/Dwr Cymru's Chief Executive. Such is the public outrage over such issues that the normally conservative *South Wales Echo* has run a campaign which contrasts his increasing wealth with the plight of those suffering automatic disconnection of water-supply by the deployment of smart-card water-meters. The *Echo* has also printed a regular update of the value of SWALEC Chairman Wynford Evans's share option package. The 'freedom' of the New Right is experienced by a tiny minority.

Unregulated behaviour in the City and Britain's financial institutions has also tarnished the image of the free market, free-for-all but without apparent effect on the dogma of a Government which sees intervention as politically unacceptable. The argument that these activities will create the wealth which 'trickles down' to improve the lives of the poor has been demonstrated to be false. In Britain, fifteen years of privatization and unregulated financial speculation have failed to create a share-owning democracy or any hint of improved incomes for the poor. In fact the opposite has occurred: 'In the last decade, the living standards of the poor and affluent marched in opposite directions. For the first time in recent years, there is official evidence that the real disposable incomes of the poorest actually fell. Between 1979 and 1988/9, the poorest tenth of the population saw their real income (after housing costs) fall by 6%; the average rose by 30%, while the richest tenth enjoyed a staggering rise of 46%'. (Oppenheim, 1993, p.1, quoting DSS sources)

The regional concentration of these financial activities has ensured that no benefits have been experienced in any of the peripheries of Great Britain and Wales has certainly seen no advantage from the 'financial revolution' of the 1980s. Indeed the privileging of the City interest in government policies throughout the 1980s severely damaged manufacturing capitalism in Britain and directly contributed to the collapse of employment in manufacturing in Wales which occurred in that decade. The most damaging of the policies was the maintenance of artificially high rates of interest in the quest to maintain deflationary pressure in the economy. The result was an eventual collapse of consumer demand and a punishing debt burden for small businesses.

The failure of liberal democracy is also its failure to create any climate in which social justice can be established. The liberal democratic conception of social justice requires society's members to be rewarded on the basis of merit. The creation of a meritocracy has been at the heart of social democratic politics in Britain since the end of the second world war. Major educational reforms, the advances of the welfare state until the early 1970s and the pursuit of full employment within the Keynesian

28

strategies of the post-war consensus, have all failed to establish the context of equal opportunities which a meritocracy requires. The fundamentally most significant determinant of an individual's outcome in life is their social class of origin. Studies from Glass (1954) to Goldthorpe (1980) have demonstrated that real vertical movement in British society remains difficult, with the division between manual and mental labour representing the most significant barrier to social mobility. The new politics must declare the meritocratic dream dead and build a more radical vision of social justice which has a sense of equality as its founding principle.

Socialist conceptions of social justice seek to combine criteria of need, equality and merit. Few socialists would advocate the creation of a society with absolute equality as its objective. However, there must be equality of need to ensure that every individual has his or her basic needs satisfied. Equality of housing, education and health-care is a prerequisite of a society in which the social exclusion and poverty discussed in this essay is abolished. Having established a basic standard of living for all, a society can create a number of criteria for establishing the distribution of additional rewards with the merit of the individual's contribution to society as the most likely qualification. There will be a requirement to limit the differential of rewards in such a society to ensure that the social system remains acceptable to all participants. In contrast to a system of social justice based on these criteria, the current philosophy of the New Right is easy to ridicule and oppose. Its claims that it preserves natural inequalities and reflects the diverse distribution of human talents has created the most unequal distribution of benefits in society since the Victorian era. The beneficiaries of the inequality are highly visible and the public is outraged at the lack of control over private wealth. Surprisingly, no one voices an alternative sense of social justice.

Strategies in the quest for the new politics must be learned from the New Right itself. Stuart Hall (Hall & Jacques, 1983) drew attention to the ways in which the Thatcherite project to create a new hegemony in British politics sought to align itself with public concerns about British society and the welfare state which were evident at the beginning of the 1980s. In a process of 'resonance' Thatcherism took those public concerns and restated them in exaggerated form and played them back to the public in an amplified reworking of the original ideas. This was especially evident around issues of rising crime and social security 'scrounging'. By deploying this strategy the Thatcher governments were able to wean the British people away from the politics of welfarism to a suspicion of the ability of the state to offer welfare support and a distaste for those who are dependent on it .

A similar strategy of resonance must be adopted in the quest for a new radical politics in Wales. Despite the major successes of Thatcherism in shifting the political ground to the right, it failed to rewrite totally the post-war settlement of the Labour years and the British public remain attached to a strong sense of communal responsibility and distrust of market forces in the contexts of health, education and housing. It is this distrust which the new politics must pick up, amplify and play back to a public which is naturally sympathetic to a critique of market forces. All classes now share a distrust and distaste for the marketization of public utilities and the public services. The new politics must address these concerns about the excesses of the application of market principles, rework them and replay them as a critique of the concept of the market itself. This is precisely the strategy adopted by the New Right in its programme of action against the welfare state. In Wales we are in a position to lead such a campaign. The New Right has never enjoyed legitimacy in Wales. The unique configuration of social forces in Wales has forced the Welsh Office to continue with interventionist strategies whilst central government moved further towards a minimalist state. The political culture in Wales has imposed a different strategy on the successive occupants of the Welsh Office and has constantly rejected the philosophy of the market-place. Unfortunately, the political opposition has done nothing to focus that dissent and give it voice. This is the task for the new politics.

Additionally, the new politics must be a popular movement in that it must resonate with popular concerns and lead popular opinion. Hall & Jacques (1983) saw one of the key features of Thatcherism as its appeal to populist trends in the political culture. Of key importance was its emphasis on authoritarianism and its successful linkage between crime, declining morality and the permissive society. This enabled an increasingly authoritarian strategy to be adopted which has culminated in the Criminal Justice Act which attempts to make alternative lifestyles and beliefs systems illegal. One of Italian Marxist Antonio Gramsci's great insights was to see that working-class consciousness has an alarming capacity to contain quite contradictory elements including fascism, liberalism, and socialism. The new politics must create a populism which feeds the socialist and collectivist components of consciousness to create a new moral system which foregrounds traditional concerns with the welfare of others. This is an important strand of Welsh culture which has not been eliminated by the New Right. However, it has been weakened and needs urgent sustenance which must come from a political movement which offers confirmation of the value and desirability of a society in which these values are celebrated.

One entry point available to the new politics into such a populist programme is through the concept of community. All political parties have appealed to the sense of community and it surfaces repeatedly in sociological studies as one of the primary sources of identity for individuals. The New Right has robbed us of a developed sense of community and reduced us to individual or family-based consumers. Where it employs the concept of community it has reduced it to an image of fortress communities under siege from the criminal and delinquent products of the permissive years. The new politics must reclaim a socialist sense of community which transcends social divisions and creates a sense of shared responsibility for all members of the community. The fear of crime must be replaced with a clear focus on the causes of crime which are, in reality, external to our communities. Unemployment and poverty can be demonstrated to be an external threat to our communities which can be opposed politically. We must diffuse the blame we place on the poor and replace it with a vivid sense of the real cause of crime. We must identify the part played by the poverty and alienation which affects those who have never worked and who subsequently lose their respect and commitment for the communities in which they live.

Finally, we must learn from the New Right that the language of politics is important. The skill of Mrs Thatcher was to use a populist vocabulary which translated complex political issues to issues of emotional appeal and created prejudice against traditional collectivist values in the community. The language of the new politics must seek to reverse this. A new rhetoric of socialism must be developed which avoids the terminology and strategy of the post-war period which is now cast into ill-repute by the New Right denigration of its purpose. We must find a new language with which to promote the core values of socialism. One potential avenue for this lies in the concept of citizenship. The ability to participate fully in society is one of the central principles of liberal democracy. If it is failing in this, as it so clearly is, it is a failed political and economic system. The sense of that failure is everywhere. In the dole-queues and the rising crime-statistics, in the urban poverty and the failure of the economy, we see its failure. The public is aware of the failure but are bombarded with messages that all is well and that the system works. Non-participation and exclusion are presented as the consequence of some personal failing. We must stress that the failure is of a political and social system and not a failure of individuals. The advantages of citizenship must be spelt out to those sections of the population who have given up on their participation and who no longer claim the right to participate. More importantly, we must raise the ability to recognize the right to participate in a generation which is growing up in a climate of social-exclusion. That generation lives in a culture which does not inform it of its rights as citizens and creates an experience which stresses the futility of attempting to participate as such.

The final component of a strategy based on the concept of citizenship requires us to consider the nature of the political unit we claim citizenship of.

One of the key components of the programme which must be adopted by any radical movement in Wales is the achievement of independence from the British state. The motivation for this claim is not only to recognize the cultural diversity of Wales but to contribute to the demise of the British Union. The existence of a United Kingdom of Great Britain is a legacy of the development of the greatest imperial power in history. The society created by the political and economic development of the British Empire is intrinsically conservative and reactionary. Indelibly stamped with militarism and monarchism, it is a society within which hierarchy and inequality are celebrated as part of the national culture. The British class-system continues to be replicated in an educational system which has the private schools on the one hand and under-funded, overcrowded comprehensives on the other. No reform of such an intrinsically divided society is possible. Fifty years of a comprehensive welfare state have failed to scratch the surface of inequalities of rank and privilege which characterize British society. The Celtic fringe has fared no better. Any claims that Scotland and Wales are more egalitarian societies are absurd. The myth of the classless *gwerin* in Welsh nationalist ideology must be dispelled by a full awareness of the divisions within Wales and their close relationship to the patterns of patronage and status operated by the British state. Breakaway from the British state is advocated because of its weakening of the power of the British state. As a consequence, all forms of devolution of power are to be supported but only as a basis for the radical transformation of the political system in which Wales exists. The erosion of the British state will permit an increasing influence from Europe where the social democratic tradition has fared a little better than in Britain during the years of the New Right and a strong socialist lobby still survives.

And now we arrive at the most difficult questions of all. Where in Welsh politics can we look to discover the source of this new radicalism which is so urgently needed? Where can we discover the moral outrage which will give it its energy? Where can we find the political will to engage in a struggle which stands against the tide of history?

Wales and the new politics

How can the new politics emerge in a Wales which has been so debilitated by the economic shifts of the global market and which has preserved itself very much in the style of the failed politics of social democracy? Can we expect a people which has been weakened by economic collapse and dispirited by fifteen years of effective disenfranchisement within an elective dictatorship to develop a new radical politics? History suggests we might. Welsh political culture is distinguished by a tradition of radicalism. That radicalism has been expressed in a variety of forms, shaped by the specific circumstances of a different era. The history of Welsh socio-political movements and events are a testimony to the influence of a comparatively small nation on the development of radicalism in Europe. The Daughters of Rebecca, the Scotch Cattle, the Merthyr Rising, the Chartists, Nonconformism, Welsh Liberalism, the South Wales Miners' Federation, the Independent Labour Party, The Labour Party, Plaid Cymru, Cymdeithas yr Iaith Gymraeg all clearly demonstrate the willingness of people in Wales to form or link to progressive social movements which swim against the political tide of their times. There is a heritage and a culture of radicalism in Wales which can be revived in the face of the scale of problems now affecting Welsh communities.

The kind of radicalism which dressed the Daughters of Rebecca or marched Chartists to Newport we can expect to have disappeared. It was the product of the maelstrom of social change in a Wales hurtling into the industrial age. The dislocation of centuries of custom and practice inevitably threw into existence a politics of violent and chaotic protest. We have no right to mourn the departure of that kind of radicalism as the social conditions which brought it into existence have matured into other less

34

evident forms of poverty and inequality. However, there is another form of radicalism which we might have expected to survive the march of Wales from industrialism to post-industrialism. The communities which coal and metal production gave birth to still exist. They are again characterized by unemployment and poverty to an extent which set a thousand feet out on the hunger-marches of the 1930s. The social conditions in our industrial towns and villages are some of the worst in Europe and the population beset by poor housing, ill health and poor education. We have a right to expect the Labour Party in Wales to be leading the reaction against this situation. But the response to this Welsh situation is a silence. A silence which drapes the Welsh Labour Party with a shroud of inaction, a silence in which the only faint sound is the rattle of mayoral chains and the polite acceptance of seats in the Lords and other forms of Tory patronage. The Welsh Labour Party takes its inspiration and its orders from Westminster. Since the second World War it has sacrificed any sense of Welsh identity and worked within the British nationalism of the British Labour Party. To understand the failure of the Labour Party in Wales we have to initially place it in this wider British context.

The first issue to establish is that the British Labour Party is itself a failure. The Labour Party in Wales is part of a fifty-year project which has failed the working-class of Scotland, England, Ireland and Wales. This failure runs much deeper than its failure to secure election for nearly sixteen years. It is a failure which pre-dates the embarrassing débâcles of the '80s and '90s. It is a failure which begins in 1945 and marks a continued failure of the British Labour movement to radically challenge the basis of capitalism. The period 1945-1953 is frequently seen as the high point of British socialism and its establishment of a social democratic welfare state. Clearly, the reforms of the period represented huge advances for the working-class of Britain. Acute poverty was gradually eradicated and the '50s and '60s can be seen as a 'golden age' of welfare protection from the excesses of capitalist economic fluctuations. However, the whole period can be seen now as a series of compromises with capitalism which allowed its continued functioning in the conditions of the world economy in the aftermath of the second world war.

Rather than a programme of radical change, the reforms of 1945 and after can be seen as a continuance of the command economy of the war period itself. Rather than a radical challenge to capitalism, the Labour settlement can be seen as creating the conditions for the continued accumulation of capital. The reforms of the period created a new basis for hegemony which recognized and incorporated the changed aspirations of the working-class which had been raised by their struggle against fascism and the associated implicit promise of their own freedom when the war was won. The apparent radicalism of the period is riven with compromises which have constituted key fracture-lines for the welfare system in the period of challenge it has faced since the late 1960s. Compromises over private education, private medicine and over the extent and nature of social ownership ensured that the welfare state had a flawed foundation which revealed itself in the ease with which the New Right have managed to roll back welfare provision.

It should not be forgotten that the twin strategies of post-war economic and social policy were the work of Beveridge and Keynes, two Liberal thinkers. The Labour vision was dominated not by the socialist ethics of the labour movement but by the reformism of the Liberal intelligentsia. At that point in history the Labour Party divorced itself from its social origins and began an ever-widening division between the Party and its grass-roots support which has culminated in the recent rewriting of Clause IV. Never again has it directly represented the interests of the working people of Great Britain but has suffered the contradictory role of attempting to ameliorate the effects of capitalism whilst creating the conditions for its advancement.

The consequences of this basic failure are enormous and are reflected in every policy failure which has beset the Labour Party in office. It renders its social ownership strategy ineffective, it creates contradictions in its taxation policy. It renders the management of the economy senseless as it attempts to serve competing objectives and it ties foreign policy continually to an essential partnership with US capital. Little wonder that every Labour Party administration in the post-war period has failed to advance beyond the welfarism of 1945. It also ensured that in the first economic crisis to face the welfare mixed economy the Labour Party presided over sustained attacks on the living standards of the British people in a disastrous attempt to sustain the 1945 dream. The post-war settlement was not socialist; it continued a sustained strategy for the management of British capitalism. It was readily accepted by the Conservative Party and ensured the survival of the class-system and British militarism. It can certainly be accepted that the commitments to full employment and the creation and expansion of a welfare state were major elements in the post-war settlement. But these co-existed with support for the international reserve and transaction roles of sterling and for a military establishment and defence task which were incompatible with an effective KWS (Keynesian Welfare State)......this reveals the hybrid and contradictory character of the postwar settlement and the limits of social democratic hegemony therein'. (Jessop et al, 1988,p. 75)

What of the Welsh Labour Party? In Wales, Labour has compounded this failure of the Labour Party to represent its natural constituency. Episodes of corruption have punctuated a permanent complacency founded on unassailable majorities. Domination of constituency politics has been matched by a strangle-hold on local authorities which has only recently been challenged in South Wales by some Plaid Cymru successes in the Labour heartlands. The security of tenure of the town halls enjoyed by the Labour Party has created a conservative and reactionary political culture which has presided over the decline of our working-class communities. Slavish acceptance of central government spending cuts and an inability to lead and to focus massive public concern over issues such as housing and education, demonstrates that the Labour Party in Wales is ideologically bankrupt and undeserving of the continued faith the majority of

Welsh people place in it. Effectively, the radicalism of the working-class communities has run out into diluted streams of a crude municipalism with its own structure of rank and privilege.

Finally, to this British and Welsh failure of the Labour Party we must add the major rightward shift which dominates the Labour Party of the present time. It has accepted the definition of the political terrain provided by Thatcherism and has spent the last ten years divesting itself of the few remaining radical elements of its agenda. This process has recently focused on the issue of reform of Clause IV which has come to represent the struggle between the small Left rump of the Party and the right-wing politics of New Labour. In our quest for a source of the new politics in Wales we must turn away from a Party which removes its beliefs in social ownership at the time when all sections of the public are most disillusioned with the politics of privatization. At no time in the last fifteen years has the electorate been more receptive to arguments for the public ownership of the major utilities. The quest for the support of the English middle-classes will ensure that the Labour Party will be unable to serve the interests of the poor in Wales or, for that matter, anywhere else.

If we are forced to reject the Labour Party as a candidate for the role of leading the new politics in Wales, where else might we look? The nationalist movement is the only other candidate. The movement represents the other strand of radicalism in Welsh history. Motivated by very different concerns from those of the Labour Party, Welsh Nationalists have demonstrated a greater willingness to pursue their objectives by radical strategies. From the burning of the Penyberth bombing-school in 1936 to the campaigns of Cymdeithas yr Iaith Gymraeg (The Welsh Language Society) nationalists have frequently employed extra-parliamentary forms of political activity to considerable effect. However, the adoption of a parliamentary strategy by Plaid Cymru has effectively divided the nationalist movement into two strands . I shall look at each of these in turn.

The first is the linguistic and cultural movement in Wales. Exemplified by Cymdeithas yr Iaith Gymraeg, this movement has continued the early concern of Plaid Cymru with linguistic and cultural survival. It is this wing of the nationalist movement which has most readily employed non-violent direct action as a device for gaining publicity and for pressing its claims against authorities in Wales. In social origin, the movement has been largely middle-class and drawn from the Welsh-speaking areas of Wales. The language activists have been characterized by their youth and there is a strong connection between the movement and the Colleges of the University of Wales at Bangor and Aberystwyth. The movement has been extremely successful in pressing its demands and gaining concessions, especially from the Welsh Office and the language has a stronger base than any of the other Celtic languages.

Despite its radical strategies, the ideology of this movement has been far from radical. At its centre is a narrow cultural romanticism which is founded on a sense of linguistic élitism and exclusion. The Welsh-speaking middle-classes have managed to hegemonize definitions of Welshness to exclude the English-speaking culture of the industrial regions of Wales and have persuaded the English-speaking Welsh of their inferiority, founded on their failure to retain the mother-tongue. The Welsh-speaking community has engineered a social division in Wales based on a sense of high and low culture in which English-speakers are defined as not-Welsh. Driven by guilt and inferiority, the English-speaking working-class of Wales flock to send their children for education in a linguistic medium which has no connection with their social world. Already disadvantaged in the education system by the dynamics of their class, the children suffer the additional disadvantage of being educated in a medium which they will never speak at home and which they will forget within three years of leaving school. A chasm exists between working-class parents and school culture in general; when it is widened by the barrier of language, the effects on the educational attainment of working-class children is catastrophic. The Welsh-speaking middle-classes have perpetrated a desperate con-trick to underwrite the survival of their language.

There has been no attempt to link the survival of the language to the economic and social vitality of the society in which it has a rightful place. Language is seen as an end in itself, with no location of the strategy for linguistic survival in a vibrant economy and society. Declarations of its socialist intent by the language movement are meaningless and the structure of the political system of Wales is of secondary importance. The Conservative administrations of the Welsh Office have recognized the importance of language concessions in defusing discontent in Wales far more readily than the Labour Party ever did and the major concessions to the demands of the vociferous linguistic minority throughout the 1980s have ensured that a potentially radical element of Welsh society has been appeased. In the meantime the poor of Wales have descended deeper into their poverty.

Finally, in our quest for a radical leadership for the new politics we come to Plaid Cymru. On the face of it we are with a strong candidate. The Party seeks independence from the British State and a relocation of Wales within Europe. This was seen earlier as an essential component of any new politics which seeks to challenge the integrity of the British state and the inequalities of class and region it maintains. Most importantly the Party has made a clear declaration of its socialist principles and its concern to organize society around a decentralist emphasis on community. Both these strategies were identified earlier as important to the formation of a new politics in Wales. Does Plaid Cymru with its articulation of a politics of socialism and community offer us the source of a radical new politics?

To answer this question we must analyze the role performed by these concepts of socialism and community within the internal structure of the Party. Plaid Cymru has historically been divided between a concern for language and culture and a concern for economic development and progress. This division has never fitted easily within a rural/urban division and there is no suggestion here that this represents a geographical division between North and South. Rather, this dichotomy represents an ideological division within the Party which we can term culturalism and modernism. Since the 1960s modernism has prevailed and the defence of language and culture has been largely left to the language movement. Despite having its primary electoral base in Gwynedd the Party has pursued a strategy which has sought increased support in the heavy industrial communities, particularly in South Wales. The culturalist elements of the Party have been able to accept this and the socialist strategy it necessitates by responding to a specific ideological appeal to their sense of community. The term community has operated as a form of social cement which has bound the disparate elements of the Party together in the 1970s and 1980s.

The concept of community employed by Plaid Cymru has never been defined and it has retained an open meaning which allows individuals to insert their own sense of community into party rhetoric. Two dominant conceptions of community have existed. The first is a sense of rural community with an emphasis on kinship, neighbourhood and identifiable patterns of language, culture and religion. The second is a sense of industrial community associated with coal and steel production, with networks of mutual aid, traditions of working-class politics and labourism. As long as the meaning of the term community was not defined, all sections of the Party could feel loyalty to a concept of decentralist socialism founded in communities. Individuals could simply insert their own commonsense meaning for the term community, derived from their particular experience of life in Wales. A farmer on the Llŷn peninsula could feel as committed to the concept as a miner from Maerdy. The concept acted as an ideological and social cement which bound the Party together and allowed the project of the modernists to proceed.

Unfortunately, in the late 1980s a solvent appeared which rapidly dissolved this ideological cement and fractured the Party along traditional fault-lines. The solvent was in the form of a perceived crisis of inward migration and its effects on the rural communities of the Welsh-speaking heartlands. Suddenly, there was a perception of threat to the very communities with which significant proportions of the Party identified. A growing awareness emerged that the modernist leadership did not necessarily share the conception of community now coming to the centre of grassroots party concerns. The symbolism of community could no longer bind the Party together and the crisis emerged as a flurry of criticism of Party chairperson Dafydd Elis Thomas. This crisis effectively revealed that the deployment of the concepts of socialism and community within the Party had never been more than an ideological device which bound it together. Community and socialism have never been carefully defined by the Party and consequently have not been built into the programme of policies it pursues. However, the concepts have been more significant than mere political rhetoric. They have been the motivating principles for many of Plaid Cymru's members, but they have not formed a coherent policy base which members can rally to. Rather, they have remained open concepts to be interpreted at will by individual members and a coherent decentralist, socialist strategy has not emerged. It is this failing which demonstrates the inability of the Party to make gains in the industrial south during the 1980s. The community socialist basis is not visible outside the Party; it has existed only as an internal mechanism of party unity.

The conclusion has to be that Plaid Cymru is riven by a contradictory need to serve both its culturalist wing and its modernist wing. This contradiction at the heart of the Party makes it impossible for it to develop a fully radical programme which could protect the communities which are the concern of this essay. The poverty and social exclusion of the industrial areas can never be fully reconciled with the needs of the rural communities, although the levels of poverty may at times coincide. The different cultural basis of the politics of these different communities makes it impossible to develop a political programme of change which serves both.

The depressing conclusion is that neither the Labour Party in

Wales nor the nationalist movement can provide the new politics required from within their present structure and programmes. Significant contradictions within both political movements render it impossible for either to step into the political vacuum experienced by the excluded and the disenfranchized poor. Both parties are wedded to strategies which limit their potential to develop a radical alternative to the pursuit of social democracy via the parliamentary process. At this stage we can begin to draw a distinction between the party mechanisms and the individual members. It is very clear that there is a growing concern in Wales for our future direction of development and an emerging popular critique of the excesses of the market economy. Assisted by a burgeoning voluntary sector which is becoming increasingly politicized, there is a rising tide of dissent which no current political organizations are giving lead to. History demonstrates that such times are likely to produce new social movements to articulate these concerns. Should this occur there are legions of discontented members and supporters of both Labour and Plaid Cymru who would constitute a natural constituency for such a movement. Additionally, there are the poor themselves who, contrary to opinion, do not simply wait passively on the sidelines of society. They are organized into credit unions, tenants' associations and self-help and community groups of all kinds. Finally, there are the articulate middle-classes who—contrary to contemporary belief—are highly capable of support for radical causes. There is a growing distaste for the kind of society we have become. Many look to the United States as a mirror of the future and wish to avoid the destination we appear to be moving towards. No one wishes to live in a society characterized by no-go areas, infringement of our ability to relax in our own communities and surrounded by fear and concern for our children. There is a constituency awaiting a radical alternative which identifies the real causes of these trends and proposes significant means of reversing them.

The requirement is for a catalyst which brings these social forces together. The most likely candidate for the role is the next

General Election. The politics of Wales remains, for the moment, bound up with the politics of Britain. An election of another Conservative Government will provide a substantial impetus for the appearance of a radicalism, especially in the Celtic fringe which has so consistently rejected such governments in the past. Equally likely is that the election of a Labour Government which is itself a pale reflection of Conservatism may spark off the same process, although a time-lag may be an additional factor. The only other likely source of inspiration is from Europe and the comparisons we as a society make with our European counterparts. Increasingly, Britain appears isolated and antiquated. Our politicians reject the levels of social provision widely accepted as the norm in Europe and we endure wages which are a fraction of European workers. We shall eventually develop an awareness of the way in which the British State stands between us and social progress of a kind accepted as inevitable in the 1960s but which has since receded to a distant memory for the population of Britain. Finally, there is a spirit abroad in the world which challenges the historical pattern of domination, located in the nation state. Small nations are claiming their right to self-determination and see themselves better served by belonging to a decentralized and federal European Union. The British State may find itself unable to sustain its grip on Scotland and Wales.

For the people who live in deprivation and suffer social exclusion the task is urgent. No one speaks for them and their own voice is ignored. More and more individuals and communities face continued decline and decay as the erosion of the welfare safety-net proceeds apace. Children are being born in Wales today into a world which will cripple their physical, intellectual and emotional development. We can no longer stand by and blame them for it.

Bibliography

David L. Adamson, (1988) *The New Working Class and Political Change in Wales*. In *Contemporary Wales* edited by Gareth Rees and Graham Day. Vol 2. University of Wales Press: Cardiff.

Benedict Anderson, (1983) *Imagined Communities*. Verso: London.

Elizabeth Bott, (1971) *Family and Social Networks*. Tavistock: London.

Norman Dennis and George Erdos, (1992) *Families Without Fatherhood*. Choice in Welfare Series, No 12. IEA Health and Welfare Unit: London.

Francis Fukuyama (1989), *'The end of history?'* The National Interest. No 16, pp. 3-18.

Andy Furlong and Fred Cartmel, (1994) *Aspirations and Opportunity Structures: Thirteen Year-Olds in Areas with Restricted Opportunities*. Strathclyde papers on Sociology and Social Policy. No 1 1994. University of Strathclyde: Glasgow.

Frank Gaffikin and Mike Morrisey, (1992) *The New Unemployed. Joblessness and Poverty in the Market Economy*. Zed Books: London and New Jersey.

D. Glass (ed), (1954) *Social Mobility in Britain*. Routledge & Kegan Paul: London.

John H. Goldethorpe, D. Lockwood, F. Bechofer & J. Platt, (1968) *The Affluent Worker: Political Attitudes and Behaviour*. Cambridge University Press.

John H. Goldthorpe et al., (1980) *Social Mobility and Class Structue in Modern Britain*. Oxford University Press.

Stuart Hall & Martin Jacques (eds), (1983) *The Politics of Thatcherism*. Lawrence & Wishart: London.

Stuart Hall, David Held andd Tony McGrew, (1992). *Modernity and its Futures*. Polity Press in association with the Open University: Cambridge.

F.A.von Hayeck, (1944) *The Road To Serfdom*. Routledge & Kegan Paul: London.

Bob Jessop, Kevin Bonnet, Simon Bromley and Tom Ling. (1988), *Thatcherism. A Tale of Two Nations.* Polity Press: Oxford.

Merthyr Borough Council, (1984) *The Way Forward. Estate Partnership. The New Gurnos.* Directorate of Community Services, Housing Services Department.

James Mitchell, (1994) *The Urban 'Underclass', Citizenship and Public Policy.* Strathclyde papers on Sociology and Social Policy. No 3 1994. University of Strathclyde: Glasgow.

Charles Murray, (1989) *Underclass.* Sunday Times Magazine November 26 .

Carey Oppenheim, (1993) *Poverty. The facts.* Child Poverty Action Group: London.

John Redwood, (1993) Speech to the Conservative Political Centre Summer School, Trevithick Building, Cardiff. July 2nd 1993. Conservative News Service.

Teri Rees & Sarah Fielder, (1992). *Smashing the Dark Glass Ceiling. Women at the top in Wales.* In *Contemporary Wales.* G. Rees and G. Day (eds). University of Wales Press: Cardiff.

Joseph Rowntree Foundation Inquiry into Income and Wealth. Volumes 1 and 2, (1995). Joseph Rowntree Foundation: York.

Unemployment Bulletin, No 22, 1986. The Unemployment Unit.

Unemployment Bulletin, No 27, 1988. The Unemployment Unit.

John Wells, (1994) *Mitigating the Social Effects of Unemployment: Crime and Unemployment .* Report for the House of Commons Select Committee on Employment. University of Cambridge.

John Wells, (1995) *Crime and Unemployment.* Employment Policy Institute. Economic Report. Vol 9, No 1. February.

Susan Williams, (1992) Social Exclusion: *The Widening Community Debate.* European Information Service. Vol 134, pp. 6-8.

Hugo Young, (1985) *Why Labour must restore faith in the future of politics. The Guardian.* March 7 p.18.

46

changing WALES